DARK DEEDS AND DESTINY

An alternative history of Haddington

By

GERALD URWIN

This book is dedicated to the memory of

Jack Tully-Jackson

WW2 local historian, mentor and friend.

CONTENTS

ACKNOWLEDGEMENTS

The author wishes to express his appreciation of the valuable assistance provided by the following sources and individuals :

1-Haddington-a history and guide (1957) Tuckwell Press

2-Feat of Arms(2002) Calder Wood Press

3- A Phoenix Once More-Librario Publ.

4-County of Haddington-(1999) John Martine

5- Ruin & Restoration (2001) Rosalind K Marshall

6- Haunted Scotland- Roddy Martine (2010)

7-A Short History of Haddington- Gray & Jamieson

8- East Lothian at War-J Tully-Jackson & Ian Brown

Plus Press reports from the Scotsman, Glasgow Herald, East Lothian Courier and Scottish daily Express.

Wikipedia

"A Vision for Haddington Town Centre"-ELC Urban Assoc.

A very special thank you to Pauline de Freitas and John Thynne for their artistic work.

Finally I must acknowledge the invaluable assistance rendered by the staff of the John Gray Centre, Haddington.

CHRONOLOGY OF EVENTS.

1548-Treaty of Haddington

1676-Ancient Fraternity of Gardeners

1688-Rev, John Gray funds a library

1748- Town House built

1770-Episcopal Church built.

1775 –(4 Oct) R. Tyne 17 feet above normal level

1817- Waterloo Bridge built

1854-Corn Exchange built.

1862-Catholic Church built.

1941- Air raid.

1948- (6-12 Aug) Tyne flood.

1949- Railway Station closes.

1973 – Renovation of St Mary's.

The author has also written :

Feat of Arms

Within these Walls

A Phoenix Once More

A Muse to Amuse

Shall Brothers Be

When Fortune Fails

Kingmaker Monck

Hard Lying

Kismet My Lady

INTRODUCTION.

Haddington's history effectively begins in 1139 when it was granted a burgh charter as a marriage gift by David 1st of Scotland to his daughter Ada de Warrenne: hence the derivation "Ada's toun" which some scholars offered as the source of the town's name, incorrectly as it later transpired.

It has always carried the basic features of a triangle resting on the banks of a river, with one arm of the triangle being the High Street and the other Market Street; Hardgate and Sidegate run along the base of the triangle.

A visitor to Haddington, in the years prior to the "Rough Wooing," (1545-49), would have acknowledged the busy nature of its occupants, for the most part engaged in going about their business which was, again, predominantly, related to the cultivation of the land around them. Each tenant was allowed a plot of land, called a "rigg," stretching behind the houses of the triangle, and on which he grew his crops and grazed his animals. The visitor would find some of these animals- pigs, geese, chickens –roaming the streets of the town and contributing to the stench thereof.

The High Street has always been commendably wide, providing sufficient space for carts and wagons to pass each other. Their clatter, allied to the baying of horses, the cries of stallholders and the sounds of busy workmen, kept the general level of noise at a high level throughout the day. Peace and quiet on the High Street arrived only after dark.

In 1138, St. Martin's Kirk was built, reputedly the oldest in Scotland. It formed part of an Abbey of Cistercian nuns founded by King William's mother, Princess Ada. The King's palace in Court Street, formerly King Street, was the birthplace of his son Alexander, later Alexander II, born in 1198.

The building of St Mary's Collegiate Church was started in the fourteenth century and completed in 1462. It replaced a former church on the same site which was destroyed by an English army under Edward III in 1356. St Mary's can lay claim to being the largest parish church in Scotland, being even slightly larger than St Giles in Edinburgh.

Haddington, in the fourteenth and fifteenth centuries, was one of the four largest towns in Scotland, with the others being Dundee, Edinburgh and Roxburgh in the Borders. Unfortunately, Haddington's geographical location placed it directly in the path of invading armies from the south which were bent on reaching Edinburgh some twenty miles away. Consequently, Haddington was invaded, sacked or burned to the ground on at least three occasions. In 1297 it was burned by a retreating Scottish army in order to deny an occupation by a pursuing English force. In 1356, as noted previously, it fell victim to a victorious Edward

III, and in 1548 it was occupied, and largely destroyed, by an English army under Lord Grey.

On each occasion, Haddington was rebuilt by its townsfolk who were determined to restore shattered lives and resume living and working in the town they loved so much. Each man's trade kept him fully occupied. It is worth remembering that moving between jobs, careers and different parts of the country was not as familiar or available as it is today.

Aberlady served as the port to Haddington. It was from there that wool, hides and other items were shipped to Europe, especially the Low Countries and Baltic ports. This trade sustained Haddington allowing it to grow and prosper. None of this commerce was to be abandoned because of the unwelcome attention of intruders: unlike Roxburgh which quickly became a desolate, deserted and ruined town once it had seen its trading port of Berwick on Tweed surrender to an English army. Roxburgh, itself was destroyed by a retreating Scottish army in a scorched earth policy.

St Mary's church lies on the east bank of the river Tyne, its architect unknown. It was built in the shape of a cross using red sandstone from Garvald and yellowish-white sandstone from Seggarsdean. It has a three storey tower which is ninety feet high and which was probably surmounted with a crown steeple in the same manner as St Giles in Edinburgh. St Mary's became a collegiate i.e. teaching church with a choir. As such it lay on the pilgrims' route from Dundee to Santiago de Compostela in Spain.

The original building had no fixed seats but benches arranged along the walls. Mass was celebrated each day at high altar and was very important to those who attended as a shield from daily vicissitudes.

Prior to the threatened English invasion in 1545, the church silver was handed over to selected individuals for safekeeping.

The various trades in Haddington vied to maintain an altar each, so that the shoemakers cared for St Crispin, the bakers St Aubert, the tinsmiths St Eloi and the tailors St Anne. There were seventeen altars in all.

Following the siege of Haddington the church was in a poor state of repair. There was no roof to the choir, or chancel, there was a lot of damage to the outer stonework, much of it still visible today, all the windows were smashed, and there was a great gap in the outer wall of the north aisle. At John Knox's suggestion a barrier wall was built in 1562 to separate the ruined part of the church from the remainder. Services could therefore resume in the nave.

In all of this time the church formed a crucial element in the lives of Haddington inhabitants. Everyone attended service and woe betide any backsliders. The church provided a solace, a reassurance to much-troubled folk but, above all. it was a source of great pride. Little wonder, then, that, whenever it was safe to do so, Haddington folk returned to their church and their town. In their view there was no other choice, certainly none worth the candle.

For a small town, Haddington has a long and important history. Perhaps no other town of its size in Scotland can compete or compare with the notable events which have taken place within its boundaries.

Nor is there any other town where so many streets have a frightening tale to tell of dark deeds and disasters!

CHAPTER ONE.

THE ROUGH WOOING.

9

Overleaf : A siege in progress.

THE ROUGH WOOING.

Without doubt the greatest disaster in Haddington, resulting in the greatest number of lives lost, occurred in the years 1548/9 at the time of the Rough Wooing. The latter term refers to the attempt, conceived by Henry VIII in 1542, to marry his son Edward to Mary, newly born in Linlithgow to Mary of Guise and James V. Henry saw it as a prime opportunity to unite the two kingdoms of England and Scotland, thus protecting his northern border and spiking the guns of the French, who were assiduously courting the Scottish establishment. To promote his aims Henry concluded an alliance with Arran, Regent of Scotland following the death of James.

Unfortuntely Arran turned out to be one of those people who must never risk giving offence, and are therefore only too ready to agree with any proposal which is put in front of them. Henry thought he had won but Arran was obliged to change his mind once he had returned to Scotland. Outraged, Henry resorted to the tactic he knew best and despatched an army to Scotland with instructions to lay waste all in its path.

In 1547 Henry died. His successor, the Regent Seymour, nevertheless pursued his predecessor's policy. He sent Lord Grey to occupy Haddington as a fortress against the Scots, who soon received massive reinforcements when a 100+ French armada sailed into Leith. Grey appointed Sir James Wilsford as commander of the Haddington garrison. Wilsford realised he had little time in which to build a defensive wall around the town, so using stone in the usual manner was not possible. Instead his troops, assisted by those few townsfolk who had remained, rapidly threw up earthworks which were substantial enough. They rose to a height of thirty feet from a base of fifty feet.

The Scottish and French armies duly arrived. The Scots made camp at Lethington (now Lennoxlove) and the French at Clerkington. They wasted no time in commencing a furious artillery barrage, firing nearly four hundred iron balls in the first day, but to no avail. Each cannonball sank into the earthworks doing little damage. At night a gleeful garrison emerged to collect all the shot they could find which they duly returned to their enemy by fire from their own batteries of guns the following day.

There followed several months of furious attack and attempts to scale the walls which were all repulsed by cannon on the four bastions, one at each corner, supported by a determined garrison. The French concentrated their fire on Wyndham's battery which held the corner of the wall nearest to St Mary's.

Eventually, having weakened the bastion to the extent that the battery of guns was withdrawn, the French staged a surprise, night-time attack, called a "camisado," and drove through a shattered gate to pour into the town itself via a narrow lane. They might have succeeded in taking the town had they not been confronted by a cannon facing them down the lane. Manning the cannon was a renegade Frenchman who had deserted a short time before. He loaded the cannon with grapeshot before opening fire. The result was devastating. Up to a hundred Frenchmen were literally blown apart. The remainder took one look at the appalling carnage and fled. The lane was running with blood and body parts lay in every direction. This lane we now know as Church Street.

Following this dreadful reverse, the French gave up any idea of storming the town walls. The Scots decided likewise, not from any fear of defeat but because another new, entirely different and altogether terrifying foe had appeared on the scene.

This foe did not assume human shape, or indeed the shape of any mammal known to man. Its shape was a complete mystery but its presence was unmistakable and quite deadly. Its reputation and its name were well known, however, and spread fear and alarm at its very mention. It was the Black Death.

The armies besieging Haddington did not surround it at first being content to set up camp to the south and west respectively. This meant that access to the port of Aberlady was still possible, which allowed supplies of food, men and equipment to reach the beleaguered garrison. These supplies came by ship. What was not known was that there was another passenger on board. It was carried by black rats, which, in turn, carried the Yersinia Pestis bacterium, a deadly pathogen.

Wilsford, meanwhile, was not content to be restricted to patrolling the walls. Instead he led several mounted forays to attack the enemy.

Such a charge on French troops on patrol outside
Dunbar Castle proved unlucky for him because
he was dismounted in the tussle and taken
prisoner. Following a transfer to Stirling he was
ransomed and returned to his home in Kent. He
died a year later as a result of the wounds he had
suffered. His successor was Sir James Acroft.
He it was who had the melancholy duty of
disposing of the corpses of those members of the
garrison, plus some of the townsfolk who had
remained, who had succumbed to the awful
plague.

The first signs of the plague were the appearance
of buboes which were inflamed swellings
usually found in the neck, armpit or groin area,
some of which grew as large as an apple or an
egg. They oozed pus and bled when opened.
They spread to all parts of the body,
accompanied by widespread black spots.
Thereafter the victim began to sweat and suffer
an acute fever. Most died within two to seven
days of infection.

Acroft's problem was how to dispose of the bodies. It was obvious to him that they could not be given a Christian burial within the confines of the town. Finally he gave instructions that the corpses had to be slung into the outer pit. Haddington was enclosed within two earth walls. The first had a deep pit at its base. The second carried the bastions (gun emplacements) at each corner as well as a deep pit on the outside. It was this pit that was chosen as the final resting place for those unfortunates who succumbed to the plague.

The plague spread rapidly in the confined space within the town walls and caused panic on all sides. Acroft realised that he needed replacements as soon as possible and despatched a messenger to the Berwick headquarters seeking urgent assistance. De Beaugue, the French commander, was content to let nature take its course and not resume any offensive. In any case his troops would very probably have rebelled against any order requiring them to even approach Haddington "where lurked the Black Death."

At his wits end, Acroft sent word to Berwick HQ "that only 1000 remain, half of the original force." A relief army of 15000 set out from Berwick. On their approach the besiegers withdrew. When all had gone, and only the burnt-out ruins of Haddington remained, Mary of Guise rode in to the town, looked around her and exclaimed "Zey av lef nozzing, nozzing but ze plague."

During the siege, Haddington's earthworks extended for about 600 metres along each side, the defences being roughly square shaped. Market Street, was used as a wall with the gaps between houses filled in with earth etc..The other sides completed the square with the river used as an additional barrier to the wall erected along its bank. The remaining two walls started at what is now Mill Wynd and ran westwards, and the final wall ran across the High Street to what is now the Town House and ended at King Street. The above calculations are only approximate and are based on what little evidence there is.

Therefore, in conclusion, the corpses were probably disposed to the south, east and west pits. None have ever been found or, at least, identified. Of course, only skeletons would remain once rats had eaten their fill.

Subsequent development of the town housing, shops etc.. has meant that no systematic investigation or digging has ever taken place. It is quite possible that some skeletons, at least, remain undisturbed beneath, Hardgate, Sidegate, Mill Wynd or even John Muir House.

CHAPTER TWO.

THE COW THIEF.

The old town of Haddington was built to allow the easy passage of horses and horse –drawn vehicles. Horses were essential to the style of living and to trading. They were prized possessions. Accordingly, any theft or attempted theft of a horse was regarded as a serious criminal offence, sometimes punishable by death.

Two examples are provided from Haddington Council records : on the 13th September 1553

Thomas Spottiswood and Mungo Alan were
accused of fighting and assault. Witnesses claim
they saw Mungo Alan attempt to
steal a horse belonging to Thomas Spottiswood
and that the two men fought with daggers and
pitchforks with Spottiswood starting the fight.
He was found guilty and Alan was acquitted.

On the 17th December 1553 James Chisholm,
bailey of Dunblane, presented a handwritten
indictment against John Robertson, accusing him
of stealing "a black nag" from Powbait Moor,
the property of Thomas Whitehead who had
been negotiating the sale of the horse. Robertson
overheard the transaction. The following
morning Robertson stole "the black nag" and
also a brown mare. Both were later found at
Robertson's home. After hearing the evidence
Robertson was acquitted, for which he was
profoundly grateful because the penalty for
horse theft was hanging.

The Tolbooth, in Market Street situated facing up Newton Port, served as Council offices, the Court of Justice and local jail. At this time the Council appointed justices to rule on legal affairs including all crimes committed within the Burgh boundaries. Penalties were invariably high and not just for horse theft. For instance: Janet Shiel has sworn an oath before the baileys of Haddington that if she is ever arrested she should be put to death.

8th July 1552. : Catherine Harrot ditto.

24th April 1553. Walter Anderson and John Glendinnan were found guilty of stealing a pair of shoes. Ordered that Walter Anderson's ear be nailed to the pillory post. John Glendinnan to be scourged and banned from the Burgh.

29th April 1553. Matthew Creyton found guilty of stealing a purse. He was sentenced to be scourged and his ear nailed to the pillory post.

7th April 1554. Matthew Robinson found guilty of stealing two pairs of shoes. He was to be scourged, his ear nailed to the pillory post, and then be banished from the Burgh. If he was ever to be arrested again in the Burgh he would be hanged.

12th October 1555. John Hey found guilty of stealing one web of cloth. He was sentenced to have his ear nailed to the pillory post and then scourged throughout the Burgh. If he was arrested again he would be hanged.

11th September 1556. John Thomson was ordered to pay Janet Darrow ten shillings as retribution for offences committed by him on her. He was to be scourged, have his ear nailed to the pillory post and then banished forever.

Scourging entailed being stripped to the waist and then lashed with a whip from the Tolbooth up Market Street, down the High Street then back along Hardgate to the Tolbooth.

17th September 1582. Janet Congilton was found guilty of stealing wool from John Manuel and Harry Burn. She was ordered to be put in the stocks and then banished.

25th January 1611. Isobel Douglas and Barbara Gray were found guilty of receiving stolen goods and were ordered to be placed in an iron bridle and collar. Any further offence would lead to scourging and banishment.

16th June 1615. William Stoddart found guilty of blasphemy and slander against the Kirk Minister. He was ordered to be placed in the stocks.

Finally, on the 27th August 1672. "A pair of stocks which stood at the bridge end were ordered to be removed.

All of which leads us to the sad tale of Jimmy Hume.

Jimmy Hume was a late unexpected arrival. His mother was already in her late thirties when he was born. It soon became apparent that Jimmy was not a normal child, being slow to learn and with something of an eastern slant to his expression. What was unknown at the time was that Jimmy suffered from Down's Syndrome, a congenital disturbance due to a chromosome defect characterised by diminished intelligence and physical abnormalities. His father died of the plague in 1550 so Jimmy's problems were linked to that fact. Jimmy and his mother were left to fend for themselves in considerably reduced circumstances. They were obliged to live in a hovel behind Bothwell Castle in the Hardgate. His mother took in dirty washing while the only work that Jimmy could find was with the stallholders in the High Street.

He was a willing worker who never refused a request or instruction. The stallholders knew not to ask him to do anything which required hard thought but instead kept him busy with simple errands, or tidying up, brushing rubbish into piles and attending horses waiting for their riders.

It was while carrying out the last of these tasks that he overheard a well-dressed lady complain to her companion "I have no milk for my child."She was, of course, referring to mother's milk and Jimmy did not hear her go on to say "so I have to hire a wet nurse." After this she turned to Jimmy, smiled at him and said "My husband will be a little while but thank you for taking care of his horse in the meantime."

Jimmy was immediately smitten by the kindness

in the remark and, above all else, the beauty of the lady whom he recognised as the Provost's wife. There and then he was devoted to her service – for life if necessary. He could not resist confiding to one of his fellow messenger boys, one Johnny Gray, and asking him where he could get some milk.

"Milk comes from a coo, you lummock." said Johnny, pointing across the High Street to a gap in the row of houses through which a herd of cows could be seen grazing in a field. Johnny saw the opportunity to play a joke on Jimmy. "There's a black coo stands by itself on the East Haugh. You could milk that."

Jimmy took the bait. He made his way down to the East Haugh on the edge of the river Tyne. Sure enough there was a black cow contentedly munching at the grass. There was no one else to be seen so he crept slowly towards the cow in order not to frighten it. He tugged and pulled up a clump of fresh green grass and held it out invitingly. The cow regarded the intruder coolly, then advanced slowly to the tempting gift on offer.

Jimmy backed away, inducing the cow to follow. He looked over his shoulder to determine the location of a barn where he was sure he could milk the cow undisturbed. He and the cow made good progress and were within a dozen metres of the barn when, suddenly, Jimmy felt a heavy hand fall on his shoulder.

"Oh no you don't, laddie. That's no your coo and you are under arrest for attempted theft."

 Jimmy looked up in surprise. With a shock he recognised the face of Bailey Craig, well known in Haddington for his tenacity in pursuing wrongdoers. Jimmy was taken roughly by the upper arm and marched off to the Tolbooth where he was flung into a dismal, dark cell.

He was terrified and unable to control his weeping. After an hour had passed his old mother was allowed in to see him. Her questions met with no coherent response despite her best efforts. At last she made to leave, giving Jimmy a final hug and kiss. Her departure only served to make him cry even louder.

Next morning, following a sleepless night and with only a drink of brackish water inside him

29

(all food having been refused by him) he came to trial. With no witnesses to speak up for him, and only his mother to plead on his behalf, it was no surprise when sentence was passed against him. It was to be carried out forthwith.

Jimmy was force marched down to the river by two burly men who each gripped one of his arms firmly behind his back. They did not halt at the river bank but walked straight into the middle of the stream. Then they ducked his head beneath the surface and held it steady. Despite thrashing as much as he could it was not long before his movements ceased and Jimmy had drowned.

A large crowd had assembled to witness the scene. Stood among them was a pal of Johnny Gray. He spotted the lady wife of the Provost. He walked up to her and quickly told her the full story of what had happened. She listened carefully, then walked over to the two men who were retrieving Jimmy's body from the river.

"I wish to relieve you of your burden, gentlemen" she said. "Here is something for your trouble" handing each a merk. They recognised her immediately, accepted her gift and handed over the corpse to her servant in waiting who was holding the reins of a palfrey. Between the three of them they contrived to sling Jimmy's body over the horse's saddle.

"And now, Jimmy, you will receive a proper burial in the church cemetery" she said, leading the way in the direction of St Mary's.

Council records blandly state

"15th October 1555. James Hume was summoned for the theft of one black cow from William Thomson's land. He was found guilty and sentence passed that he be taken to the Tyne and drowned."

Jimmy Hume is taken to the river.

CHAPTER THREE.

THE SLAYING OF OLD JOHN.

Overleaf : Old John's farm.

The Court in the Tolbooth on 15th June 1580.
The following case was heard :

John and Alexander Henryson appeared before
the Court and were accused of the slaughter of
John Stevenson by his son, also called John, by
open proclamation at the Market Cross. The
Provost and baileys were deemed competent to
judge the case, under the new Commission ,
granted by the King's Grace. John and
Alexander Henryson were therefore summoned
by indictment for the alleged slaughter of the
late John Stevenson and were required to appear
before the Assize.

Members of the Assize were John Douglas,
Robert Byres, Paul Lyle, Adam Wache, Andrew
Thomson, Patrick Hogg, William Douglas and
Archibald Kyle. The date for the hearing was
fixed for the 23rd November in the Tolbooth in
Market Street.

The proceedings begin with the Provost rising to
his feet and declaring "By the authority invested

in me as Provost of this fair Burgh of
Haddington, I, Robert Nesbit, summon all
present to hear the case for the accusation of
murder brought against the accused, that justice
might be done and be seen to be done by one
and all. Bring forth the prisoners."

Two men, dressed only in shirt and pantaloons,
barefoot, and with their hands tied behind their
backs, are brought into the body of the court by
two men dressed as town militia

The Provost speaks again. "Almighty God, give
us this day the wisdom we need to find the truth,
that we may serve thee as we ought. And may
we be fair to all who are brought before us and
work to thy infinite mercy. In the Name of the
Father, Son and Holy Ghost. Amen."

Provost "Who stands for the accused?"

Four men stand to shout out their names in
turn."Henry Balfour. William Hay. John Provan.
Andrew Home."

Provost. "Who stands to accuse?"

Four men shout out their names in turn.

"John Stevenson. Alexander Brown. Michael Forrest. Thomas Stevenson."

Provost."Does either of the accused confess his guilt?"

John Henryson answers "In God's name, not I."

Alexander Henryson answers "Nor I, in God's name."

Provost." Let it be known, to all present and beyond, that this day we give trial to the accused by the gracious permission of the Commission of the King's Grace, in whose name we serve. The victim of this cruel and bloody crime was a respected dweller in the Burgh, a burgess and a freeman. Nor was there any man more esteemed. Therefore, I say to you, truth and justice will be sought and secured, that he might rest in peace in his grave, and that by your peers shall you, the accused, be truly judged. Let the trial proceed."

John Stevenson. " Step forward, Michael Forrest, and tell your tale."

Michael Forrest. "Twas the night the cordiners gathered at the tavern by Market Cross to complain of the theft of the box pennies on February the seventh, I trust. I saw John and Alexander Henryson sitting in the corner. I thought it was strange, because they were the only ones there who were not cordiners that night. When I asked them why? They told me they were waiting for old man Stevenson. Alexander Henryson said they were going to have a reckoning, but would not say on what account. Later, I heard that old Stevenson had agreed to sell them some land, but had changed his mind, although others claim it was not the land they were after so much as the two horses that graze on it."

John Stevenson "And do others pledge your tale is true?"

Alan Brown and Thomas Stevenson "Aye. True it is."

John Stevenson "Step forward, Alan Brown, and tell your tale."

Alan Brown " Be it known that I was leaving the house of Molly Simpson, where I had restored the roof. I am a slater and tiler, my Lord Provost. It was the eve of the day before the body was found, so that must have been April 15th. I saw two men running hard down Lydgate. That's where Molly Simpson bides. They were coming from the direction of old John Stevenson's home. They were both in a panic, looking back to see if they were pursued, and one of them still had a quinzer in his hand. It was dripping with blood."

John Stevenson "Who were these men?"

Alan Brown "I swear, by my dear mothers' grave, it was the Henryson brothers."

John Stevenson "Thomas Stevenson. Step forward and tell your tale."

Thomas Stevenson "I heard my father, at times, speak in strong displeasure of the Henryson brothers, calling them arrogant, angry and violent.

John Stevenson steps forward. "And so did I. Let it be known that there never was a son who loved his father more dearly than I. To see him lying there, dying on a stone cold floor, was enough to chill the blood. I swore revenge while kneeling at his side, and, as God is my judge, revenged I shall be. But, to begin on the morning before that fateful day, I left my father, cheerful and healthy, and rode to Aberlady where I had business with Captain Mitchell of the craft "Rose," newly arrived from Hamburg with a load of timber, pottery and vegetables. We dined aboard ship, and it was mid-afternoon ere I

returned to Haddington. After drinking with
friends at the Star tavern, I betook myself to my
lady's house where I reclined and slept. I woke
early in the morn and made my way to my
father's house, intending to invite him to dine
with me that day, but, as I neared the stables, I
heard a piteous groaning, the groaning of a man
in dire straits, a sound that froze the very
marrow in my bones. To my horror, I came upon
a sight which will live with me to my dying day,
that of my own dear father, lying on his side on
the ground, covered in blood, groaning and
trying to rise. I rushed to him and held him in
my arms while deciding what best to do. He lay
and looked up at me in a piteous way.

"Father, dear father, who could have done this to
you?" I cried.

He whispered only one word, then fell back
dead. That word was "Henryson."

Provost "Remove the prisoners to their cell. We
shall take a recess lasting one hour."

RECESS.

All return as before.

Provost. " Untie the prisoners and bring them forth."

The two prisoners are brought in by the guards and their hands untied.

Provost. "Who is it that will speak for the prisoners?"

Harry Balfour. "Not I."

William Hay. "Nor I."

John Provan. "Nor I."

Andrew Home." Nor I also."

Provost. "Is there none to speak for the prisoners?"

John Henryson. "Since no one will speak for my brother and I, then I will do so. There remain questions to be answered."

Provost. "John Henryson will speak for the prisoners."

John Henryson. "Then step forward, Michael Forrest."

Michael Forrest steps forward.

John Henryson. "You claim you saw us in the tavern by Market Cross on February seventh, did you not?"

Michael Forrest. "Aye, I saw you plain."

John Henryson." You asked my brother why we were there and he told you we awaited old John Stevenson, did you not?"

Michael Forrest. "Aye. So I affirm."

John Henryson. "The cordiners spoke loud and long, did they not. They were not wishing to overlook anything?"

Michael Forrest. "Aye."

John Henryson. "So they were all present in the tavern for a good while.?"

Michael Forrest. "Aye. Until the landlord asked us to leave for fear the watch would come."

John Henryson. "And tell us. Were my brother and I also present?"

Michael Forrest. "Aye. It's true. The two of you were there until the end."

John Henryson. "Why would that be? My brother and I are not cordiners."

Michael Forrest. "As I said before. The two of you were there to meet old John Stevenson."

John Henryson." And did we?"

Michael Forrest. "Aye. He was talking to you."

John Henryson. "Did he also stay until the end?"

Michael Forrest. "I think not. He left before the others."

John Henryson. "In what fettle?"

Michael Forrest. "What do you mean?"

John Henryson. "Was he in a rage? Was he shouting?"

Michael Forrest." No. He left quietly enough."

John Henryson. "Then was he smiling? Was he a happy man?"

Michael Forrest. "As far as I could tell."

John Henryson. "My brother, then, could not have spoken harshly to him. I ask that my brother, Alexander Henryson, step forward."

Alexander Henryson steps forward.

John Henryson. "Tell the Assize, and all here, what was said that night."

Alexander Henryson. "We talked calmly, man to man."

John Henryson. "What did you talk about?"

Alexander Henryson. "I asked old John to sell us twelve acres of good land, land that lies off Lydgait and was once Ralph Eglin's acres."

John Henryson. "And did he accept?"

Alexander Henryson. " Aye. Indeed he did. He said that he knew we were of good farming stock and would make good use of the land."

John Henryson. "Why should he say that?"

Alexander Henryson. "Because he knew no good would come of it if he left it to his eldest son."

John Henryson. "What did he say of his eldest son?

Alexander Henryson. "He called him a wastrel spendthrift and a bully braggart who would ruin the family name."

John Stevenson interjects. "Full five and twenty years have I dwelt in this Burgh and always in my father's house. Who is there who knows me who would claim such as this wretch does? What man is there who would deny the truth, as God is my judge, that my father and I were dear to each other? Who, but a desperate waghorn, would deny the love between father and son? By such a contumely he condemns himself and his brother out of his own mouth."

Provost." Would you ask further, John Henryson?"

John Henryson. "Indeed sire. Alan Brown. I pray you step forward.

Alan Brown steps forward.

John Henryson. " Tell true if you will. Did you not say that you saw my brother and I the night of April 15th?"

Alan Brown. "So I did. So did we both."

John Henryson. "Who saw the same as you?"

Alan Broan. "Why, Molly Simpson. I was at her house."

John Henryson. " Standing at the port, I trust?"

Alan Brown. "No. Not at the port. At the winnock we stood."

John Henryson. " At what hour of the night was this?"

Alan Brown. "I know not the hour – but late on."

John Henryson. "And where stood my brother and I ?"

Alan Brown. "Why, on the far side of the Lydgait, but not standing but running hard."

John Henryson. " And does the port of Molly Simpson's house open straightway on to the Lydgait?"

Alan Brown. "Oh no! Of course not. Why such a house must have land both to front and rear."

John Henryson." Then, sire, do you tell true to say that late on the night of April 15th, when - sun had long gone from the sky, while you stood

at the winnock with Molly Simpson at her home
in the Lydgait, you saw, beyond the land that
lies to the front of the house, beyond the stretch
of Lydgait – and running! –my brother and I."

Alan Brown. "Oh aye. I did. We both did. And
he was carrying a quinzer."

John Henryson. "Who, sire?"

Alan Brown. "What do you mean?"

John Henryson. "Who, sire, did you see carrying
a quinzer ? Was it my brother or myself?"

Alan Brown. " E-eh. It was you – I think. No.
twas the brother. Yes your brother>"

John Henryson. "And all that you saw plain as
day?"

Alan Brown. "Er. Yes. No –at night"

John Henryson. " So if I ask you to pick out my
brother-who you saw plain as day – out of the

49

group of men standing over there at the far side of the court room, you could do it?"

Alan Brown. "Er. Yes. I think so. Tis yon man at the far end, is it not?"

John Henryson. "No sire. It is not. My brother stands in the middle. Step forward."

Alexander Henryson steps forward, smiling.

Alan Brown is dismissed.

John Henryson. "Yet are we any nearer the truth if it. The time of the slaying is still in doubt. One says "night" but cannot see true. The other says "day." Who can we believe?"

John Stevenson. "I have told true. My father died in my arms on the morn."

John Henryson. "Then how could my brother and I have slain him the night before? He could not have lain alive all night. And where were you at the time of the slaying? You claimed you were at your lady's house. Where is the truth of it? Will the lady speak for you?"

John Stevenson. "Ask away. You will not hear her name from my lips."

A smart, well-groomed lady steps forward from the crowd.

"I am she who you seek."

Provost. " Let it be known it is Mirren Black who speaks. Tell us, dear maid, all you know to add to the truth. Did John Stevenson, the younger, come to you on the night in question?"

Mirren. "He did indeed."

John Henryson. "Do you have proof?"

Mirren. " He left his sark and asked me to wash it."

(She holds a sark to her which displays the Stevenson crest, at which point John Stevenson turns his back to display the identical crest.)

John Stevenson. "There you have it. All the proof you need. I was there that night as the crest shows."

John Henryson. "And why, pray, should you ask to have it washed?"

John Stevenson. "My lady asked for a keepsake and the sark was all I had with me that I could spare."

Mirren. "I have not finished my tale. A pretty sark it is, sire, and a pretty tale you tell. But there are two sides to the tale - and two to the sark."

(She reverses the sark to expose the front of it. It is covered in bloodstains.)

Mirren. "I sought no keepsake from John Stevenson, nor would I for he is nothing to me. He did come to me that night. Not as any bold suitor, but white-faced and gasping, pleading for me to wash the blood from his sark. I see now, which I did not then, that it is the blood of his own father, slain by the hand of a vengeful son. Fate and experience told me not to wash the sark, lest another would suffer, even though he threatened me and my own dear father in the vilest and most blood-curdling terms. When I heard that the Henrysons were to stand accused of the slaying of old John Stevenson, I could not bring myself to wash the sark. All this I tell true."

Provost. "Thank you my lady. (turning to John Stevenson). Is it the truth? Did you slay old John Stevenson, your own father?"

(John Stevenson turns to flee but the guards hold him fast. He sags visibly, then turns to face the Provost.)

John Stevenson. "For three hundred years have the Stevensons lived on this land. In all of that time they have been among the most respected of all. They have toiled, prospered and grown rich, yet have they also not given? Aye, indeed. Given of their time, their skill, their effort, their advice and their riches. All to Haddington and its people. Is there any man among you who has not cause to bless the name of Stevenson? To be born in such a family I take to be the greatest honour. To succeed and lead them was all that I planned, yet my own dear father put all this at risk. How could he come to sell Stevenson land –my land? How could any man of honour stand by and do nothing but watch his hopes for the future, and his right, be dashed? I pleaded with him and told him of my plan, of my love for him and my duty as a son and heir. But he gave no regard to any of it. He insisted that the land would be sold. The unkindest cut of all was when he told me to leave his house and leave Haddington, saying I would never be the man he was and should seek my future elsewhere, since my name would not appear in his will. In the end I slew him as the only way."

Provost. "Take him away. We shall sentence him tomorrow."

Two guards seize John Stevenson and bundle him off to the cells.

GLOSSARY.

Quinzer – a dagger

Waghorn – a great liar – the Devil Himself.

Winnock – a window.

Sark – shirt.

Cordiner – shoemaker.

55

CHAPTER FOUR.

THE STANFIELD MURDER.

Below : the Mill Wheel.

THE STANFIELD MURDER.

Sir James Stanfield fought for the New Model Army under Oliver Cromwell and was attached to General George Monck's regiment in Scotland.Following the Restoration of Charles II he made his home in Edinburgh, in World's End Close overlooking the Netherbow Port. Stanfield proved to be a shrewd businessman who soon acquired a reputation for helping out less fortunate noblemen with their financial affairs. Stanfield was also interested in becoming a landowner and bought land in Leith. Later he moved to East Lothian, buying an estate at New Mills. Soon he had started up a waulk (thick cloth) mill spreading to other mills along the Tyne on land formerly belonging to the Abbey of Haddington. The company he formed was called the New Mills Cloth Manufactory. It housed twenty looms and produced 50,000 metres of cloth, which gave a profit of over £16.000 (approx. £125,000 in modern times.)

The company ran succesfully for twenty years on a more or less successful path, although a shortage of suitable local labour meant skilled workers had to be brought in from England and elsewhere. By 1654 over 700 were employed, and Stanfield was knighted for his efforts. Stanfield, however, had severe psychological problems and had a reputation as a melancholic. In one instance, he was only prevented from pitching himself headfirst out of the window by someone clutching at his heels.

On a day near the end of November 1687,Stanfield was found drowned in the

Tyne. As a melancholic it was at first assumed that he had committed suicide. People became suspicious at the somewhat hasty funeral, along with the fact that a grave cloth had been prepared in readiness some time before. Philip Stanfield, the son, who had claimed to find his father's body, was accused of his murder when his father's body bled copiously after he had touched it.

Philip Stanfield was brought to trial on February 6th, 1688. Although his father had ensured that he had a sound education, he had fallen into bad ways and was guilty of debauched, villainous behaviour. He was constantly being detained in prisons all over Europe, including Antwerp, Orleans, and London.

An exasperated Sir James had signified his intention to disinherit him in favour of his second son, John Stanfield, whereupon Philip had declared his intention to kill his father.

He had indeed chased him on to the highway
and fired at him.

On the 7th July 1688, at Edinburgh court,
witnesses testified to Philip swearing to kill
any man who opposed him. His fellow
conspirators, Janet Johnston, George
Thomson and his wife, were also charged.
They all testified that they had frequently
heard the accused curse his father, saying that
he had hated him "these seven years".

On the Friday before Sir James's death, Janet
Johnston spent a long time with the victim in
his chamber. She found Sir James subdued
following an argument with his wife. Janet
went to light a fire in Sir James's chamber on
the following morning and found the bed
already made up, with the candle, which was
normally at the bed head, was, instead, at the
foot. The accused ordered the body to be
taken to his cellar "for he died more like a
beast than a man." He entered his father's

study and took gold and money.He removed
the buckles from his father's shoes and put
them on his own.

James Morehead, a surgeon, testified that,
when the accused assisted in lifting the body
of his dead father, it poured out blood
through the covering linen from the left side
of the neck which the accused had touched.

James Thomson declared that Janet Johnston
came to his father's house before ten o'clock
on the night Sir James met his end. Philip
Stanfield arrived shortly after. Conversation
was held in whispers between Philip, Janet
and George Thomson, James's father. Philip
was heard to complain his father kept him
penniless and "God damn his soul if he
should not seek an end of his father." Then
all would be his and he would remember his
friends.

James Thomson heard his parents go out of
the house but return after an hour and a half

saying "the deed was done." They carried him to the edge of the river and tied a stone around his neck, but later removed it before throwing the body into the river.His mother assured his father that "it will be thought he drowned himself." When the body was found next morning his mother roused his father "If you are found in your bed they will say you had a hand in the murder."

Janet Johnston's daughter, Anne Mark, said that on the night Sir James was killed his son, the accused, came to her mother's house seeking George Thomson and his wife. She was told to go and see if Sir James had returned home. When she confirmed his return the accused ran off to New Mills. At 11 p.m. her father sent her to fetch her mother. She found her with the accused at George Thomson's house. Her mother stayed on, not returning home until two in the morning. Her father cursed and demanded to know where she had been. She replied "Where I have been the deed is done."

The jury found the accused guilty of all in the indictment, from cursing to being an accessory to his murder. He was ordered to be hanged at Edinburgh Cross on the 15th February and his tongue cut out. His right hand would be cut off and his head hung at the East port of Haddington. The remainder of his body would be hung in chains between Leith and Edinburgh. All his lands and goods were confiscated.

CHAPTER FIVE.

THE FLOOD.

Overleaf : The river pre-flood.

CHAPTER FIVE.

THE FLOOD.

The river Tyne rises in the Moorfoot hills near
Tyne Head in Midlothian. For most of its
journey to the sea it runs thirty miles through
East Lothian in a north easterly direction. It
enters the North Sea at Belhaven near Dunbar.

For most of the year the river flows quietly
through Haddington, and the banks of the river
offer an idyllic setting, ideal for picnics,
exercising the dog. or just strolling idly along
the haughs (riverside meadows). It is a shallow
river for the most part as it flows through
Haddington and easily fordable. There still
remains a ford which lies below the old Nungate
bridge. The ford was previously much used by

carts, wagons and horses before the bridge was built. The bridge, built of red sandstone, is cobbled and quite narrow being only fourteen feet wide, while it extends for over two hundred feet. It probably dates from the late fifteenth or early sixteenth century. A notable feature is the iron L-shaped hook projecting from the wall of the bridge on the west side of the river. Reputedly this hook was used to dangle criminals and wrongdoers just above the surface of the river. The bridge has three arches, suggesting that the river was at one time much wider before silting up.

The stretch of river which runs through Haddington is a haven for birds, ducks and swans. The cob swan fiercely contests his beat, keeping all at bay. Ducks, dogs and small boys have all fled in terror from his loudly flapping wings. Hen swan sails majestically up and down the river, leading her family of (usually) six or seven cygnets in search of food.

This seemingly everlasting scene of tranquillity is only occasionally disturbed. In autumn, in particular, when rainwaters flood down from the hills, the river takes on a different character altogether.

Then it becomes a raging torrent, sweeping away all in its path and spreading widely over the surrounding countryside, inflicting heavy damage.This has been a pattern for centuries past.

For instance : Haddington Council records for the 15th September, 1599 state – "at 12 midnight a great flood swept from the Tyne up to Robert Duncanson's stair, and then on to the crest of the highway near the Tron, and then into the gutters at the Cross...the dam wall collapsed after the flood, and all of the sluices, except one at the east end of the water gate, were swept away...the bridge end, which had collapsed, would also have to be repaired."

The Bell Inn, situated half way up Haddington's High Street, was a thriving hostelry throughout the seventeenth, eighteenth, and even into the nineteenth centuries. Its central location ensured a steady supply of customers, but the fact that it became a coaching inn guaranteed success. The coach from Edinburgh stopped at the Bell Inn to change horses. Hungry passengers could satisfy their eating and drinking needs and be sure that everything was waiting for them. For a coaching inn to allow delays of any description would have been disastrous all round. There were other inns in Haddington eagerly waiting their turn.

The Bell took its name from its owner, Thomas Bell and his wife, daughter and two sons were all employed there. Wife Hester and daughter Helen were kept busy in the kitchen while the two sons, William and Adam, served as ostlers, hotel manservants and barmen. Adam, the younger, was not averse to helping himself from behind the bar counters. The accumulation of drininkg throughout rhe day caused him to lose his sobriety on more than one occasion. Despite warnings from his father, his behaviour did not improve. Several customers complained to Thomas that his son was, at times, unruly and threatening. Inevitably, one confrontation with a customer got out of control and a fight started which saw a town bailey and a constable summoned. Adam appeared in court and was fortunate to be merely warned as to his future conduct, probably due to the high regard in which his father was held in the Burgh.

On Wednesday, the third of October, 1775, the heavens opened and it poured with rain for the whole day. Two mail coaches arrived at the Bell almost simultaneously. One came from Edinburgh and the other from England on its way to Edinburgh. The Bell was heaving with customers, not only from the two coaches but also from many locals seeking refuge from the elements. Nobody was in any hurry to leave.

Thomas and his family strove to keep everyone happy and well supplied with food and drink. For once Adam was too busy to stop for a drink, which probably did not help him to keep his temper. There appeared to be no let up in the demands made by the huge crowd of customers. It was inevitable that Adam's temper would snap at some stage. The crucial moment came when a man, himself obviously inebriated, and who was a stranger to Adam, claimed he had not been served with his latest order, and had been waiting for too long. Adam, who was busy serving another with a large drink order, muttered something by way of explanation, which failed to satisfy the complainant. He grabbed Adam's arm, causing him to spill a tray of tankards and pint pots, all full to the brim. Adam's face went red and he swung the empty tray against the man's head. Blood flowed and mayhem ensued.

A bailey and constables were summoned and Adam was marched off into custody to await trial the following day. He was held in an underground cell in the bailey house. The cell served as a waiting room for prisoners due to appear in the Court House next door, and was situated at the top of the High Street, not one hundred yards from the Bell Inn itself.

Overnight the storm continued. The level of the Tyne rose quickly. The sluices were soon blocked by uprooted trees and other debris. Before long the river had overlapped its banks. It spread into town, climbing steadily up both Market Street and the High Street. Stallholders and shopkeepers tried desperately to halt the inevitable progress of the flood but to no avail.Soon they gave up the unequal struggle and fled. The water flowed inexorably up the High Street. Those employed at the Court House and the baileys' room nearby opted to flee also.

Meanwhile, Adam Bell, confined to his underground cell, could hear the commotion of raised voices calling out in alarm. He shouted out himself but no answer came. At first water started to drip into his cell from the barred window which was free of glass. Thoroughly alarmed, he banged on the door of his cell and again shouted for help. There was no response. All had fled.

The water rose quite rapidly in his cell. Soon it was up to his knees. Desperately he looked around his cell, seeking an escape, but there was none. Panicking, he screamed for help as loud as he could and pounded the door in frustration. The water was now up to his waist. He was finding it difficult to maintain his footing and stay upright. Trying to stay calm despite his plight he felt that surely his family would realise the peril of his situation and come running. All of his efforts proved fruitless. There was no sound other than that of the water rising, in its inevitable way, above him. It was now chest high. He scrambled to hold on to the edge of his cot, trying desperately not to slip beneath the surface. At the last panic overwhelmed him and all he could do was scream.

The following day the storm had passed and the river had ceased to spread. By the end of the day it had receded to the lower end of the town, leaving the main thoroughfares passable. Gradually townsfolk returned to their houses, shopkeepers and stallholders to their property and court officials to their place of work. Too late the constable remembered that there had been an overnight prisoner in the holding cell. He hurried to the cell door and unlocked it. Immediately he was swept from his feet by a deluge of water released as he opened the door. Spluttering, he regained his footing. His composure restored, he peered inside the cell.

Lying on the cell floor was the body of a man, eyes staring into space and a look of horror on his face upwards to the cell ceiling. Adam Bell was dead. He had drowned in his cell.

Years later, the new tenant of the property, now in private hands, discovered the old cell below ground. He took a lamp with him to look around. Running across the ceiling was a series of scratch marks as if someone had dug his nails into the ceiling plaster in a mad frenzy.

The Tyne restored to a calmer mood.

CHAPTER SIX

ST MARTINS.

Overleaf : The ruins of St Martins.

ST MARTIN'S.

The Cistercian Abbey, founded by Countess Ada
de Warrenne, in 1178, was sited a mile to the
east of Haddington. The only remaining trace of
the abbey is the ruined chapel of St Martin's in
Nungate, thought to be the oldest surviving
church in Scotland, even older than its sister
church, St Mary's, which stands nearby on the
river Tyne.

A strange historic link between the two churches
centres around the aftermath of the Siege of
Haddington, 1548-9. During the siege the
English gunners deliberately avoided firing on
either kirk until it was seen that Queen Marie of
Guise, and her party of courtiers, were about to
climb up to the bell tower of St Marys in order
to observe the struggle between besieged and
besiegers. This was seen as a provocation and

caused the English force to open fire, killing many of the French party but not Marie herself, who made a hurried escape.

One of her party, Sieur Pierre Michel de Chateau d'Orgny, Marquise de L'Evreux, had hurried forward ahead of the Queen's party, and eventually reached the bell tower of St Marys. Clothed in white from head to foot he was quickly spotted and immediately fired on. A cannonball took off his head and his headless corpse plunged downwards. Legend has it that it screamed as it fell. Thereafter it is alleged that his ghost wanders between the two kirks as if searching for something it has lost.

In the years following the siege, troops have continued to be billeted in Haddington on an almost permanent basis. Council records, over hundreds of years, make a continued reference to soldiery.

For instance : on the 13th June, 1659, it is noted "...a discussion took place on the problem of seeking new quarters for soldiers, whose horses were supposed to graze outwith the Burgh, or else to agree a sum of money to be paid to the landlords, in the hope that it would be repaid by the soldiers." Presumably this reference is to soldiers of General Monck's occupying army, prior to them marching south to England and the Restoration of the Monarchy.

On the 8th September, 1659 it is noted "The Provost, James Forrest and David Kyle, were chosen to pay a visit to General Monck, to see if a quarter of the troops, stationed in Haddington, could be moved elsewhere."

On the 17th March, 1689, is recorded "...in order to repair the damage caused by two regiments of foot soldiers (Colonels Hastings and Leslie) all persons wishing to make a claim were instructed to inform the Clerk (of Works)."

On the 5th January, 1691 "... the Magistrates and Committee for the scrutiny of the accounts, allowed the following:

1) –an account due to John Smyth amounting to £133/19/10d for money spent in entertaining the officers of the battalion of Lieutenant General Douglas's regiment.

2) –the Council allowed an account for £60/1s. for coal provided to the Guards Regiment of Patrick Fleming.

On the 6th August, 1692 "The Treasurer was instructed to pay residents of the Burgh their cart and horse hire, for removing the Army's baggage and ammunition last winter."

On the 1st December 1694 "The Council allowed payment of an account, amounting to £80/14/6d for transporting the regimental baggage of Colonels Buchan, Cunningham and Douglas..."

Finally, on 8th May, 1709, included in a lengthy petition to "His Gracious Majesty, High Commissioner and Right Honourable Members of Parliament" there are the following items : the Commissioners of the Army are obliged by law to keep magazines of corn and straw for the Dragoons...when the said Dragoons were marching through the Burgh...the said Commissioners neither kept any magazine of corn and straw, or paid our people the current rate of the country. Whereas our burgesses and inhabitants could not provide these Dragoons' horses a night's corn and straw under 16s., whereby our people were paid only 5s, thereby losing 11s. per horse per night."

Later, in the same document, the Council ordered the following instructions :

-to vote for reducing the army.

- to vote for taking course to see how the people of Haddington might be reimbursed by the Commissioners of the Army for providing corn and straw to the Dragoons...at the said Commissioner's rate.

Artillery Field, in north east Haddington, is named after the site of the Artillery Corps temporary building, erected in the late nineteenth century for lodging.

In the autumn of 1810, with Britain still at war, with Napoleon's French army still possibly planning an invasion, the 35th Royal Sussex Regiment of Foot, comprising 326 cavalry officers, 800 artillery troops, and 1158 infantrymen, were housed in camp in Haddington.

With little or nothing to occupy their minds, it is of little surprise that mischief, of one type or another, would eventually break out among officers and men. A Doctor Cahill rebuked Captain Hugh Blair Rutherford about the general state of well being of the men under his command. In effect, he claimed that lack of physical exertion was leading to outbreaks of gambling and drinking which were much above the norm.

Not surprisingly, the Captain was outraged, and strongly denied the accusation. The dispute between the two grew louder and stronger. Neither was prepared to withdraw his statements or stance. Inevitably a duel was called as the only means to resolve the issue. Both men took their place in a field outside the camp, raised their pistols and fired. The twenty four old Captain Rutherford fell mortally wounded. His assailant, Doctor Cahill, rushed to his side to render what medical service he could offer but to no avail. The proud Captain soon expired.

Following the incident great remorse was shown on all sides, not least by the Captain's own men who were very fond of him. He was buried in the graveyard of St Martin's Chapel with a large crowd in attendance. His fellow officers gathered together to seek solace in drink. All too soon they were suffering from the effects of imbibing a copious amount of wine. Voices were raised, vows made, all culminating in a foolish wager struck whereby one Lieutenant Grey, a great friend of the deceased, declared he would visit the corpse's grave at midnight and plunge a dagger into it, as a form of protest, and to show his personal grief.

As a protection against the cold night, the lieutenant put on a large cloak before marching off to the grave in St Martin's yard. He found the grave he was looking for and plunged his dagger downwards. In doing so he drove through the voluminous swirl of his cloak, effectively pinning himself to the ground. Befuddled and cursing, he struggled to free himself. His attention was distracted by some movement at the other end of the graveyard. To his horror he saw a ghastly white apparition moving slowly in his direction.

The apparition moved slowly from side to side as if in search of something or someone. Grey watched open-mouthed, his wide in horror, as the figure approached. He gasped as he realised that it had no head. The old story of the siege came to him.

"Tis the ghost of Sieur Pierre Michel de Chateau d'Orgny, Marquise de L'Evreux who seeks his head," he whispered.

The figure came nearer, and nearer – and nearer.

His friends, meanwhile, had continued with their revelry and drinking for several hours. At last, one of them reminded his fellow officers that Lieutenant Grey had not returned. They progressed slowly to the graveyard, carrying lighted torches to see their way. One of them cried "There he lies, yonder!" and rushed forward. The others followed to find the lifeless body of Lieutenant Grey beside their former comrade's burial plot. His eyes were open, as wide as they could be, a look of abject horror on his face.

CHAPTER SEVEN.

SCOTTISH FENCIBLES.

89

Overleaf : an East Lothian "fencible."

In 1793 Great Britain and France were at war with each other once again. The latter had a considerable advantage militarily, in that its army was large, well established, and already very successful in the field. Should France decide to invade, it would surely brush aside any opposition which could be brought against it. The time was ripe, if not already overdue, for raising a volunteer army which could defend the British Isles. Such a force would make Britain "defensible," and so it was almost inevitable that the troops raised would become known as "fencibles." Spirits were raised and fists shaken eastwards i.e. towards France.

The "fencibles" were therefore the forerunners of the Home Guard (originally known as "Local Defence Volunteers") which was raised in 1940 against possible invasion by Germany. They would serve until such time as they were no longer needed, and could therefore release regular troops to fight abroad. In Scotland they would be the first countrywide militia ever raised.

The 1st March, 1793, saw the appointment of seven Colonels of Fencible Regiments in Scotland. As before, from time immemorial, these Regiments were formed locally as if at the command of a clan chief. Most recruits came from the area where they were tenants, with many familiar names in their regimental titles, such as the Campbells in Argyll, the Sutherlands in Sutherland, and Gordons in the north. The same applied to Fencible cavalry, such as the Linlithgow troop raised by a Livingston, and Lothian units raised by a Kerr or a Hamilton.

The organisation of a Scottish Fencible Regiment saw one Colonel, one Lieutenant Colonel, one Major and five Captains. Each Company had one Lieutenant, one Ensign, three Sergeants, four Corporals, three drummers and 71 privates. An enlistment bounty was fixed at three guineas. Pay and allowances were the same as for the regular army.

In East Lothian Haddington Fencibles were raised as volunteers in 1795 to repel invasion and protect property. 1796 saw the first encampment which was erected at West Barns. It became the largest in the east of Scotland.

The uniform adopted by local "fencibles" was a scarlet jacket, laced with green and white lace, with (usually) white breeches. Each man carried a musket and was also given a haversack and canteen. Drill took place twice a week, on Wednesdays and Saturdays.

Captain Quentin Darnley was in a foul mood. He sat on his horse watching a squad of volunteers firing at wooden targets at a distance of one hundred yards. His expectations and hopes lay in ruins. His early motivation to join the army as a serving officer in the face of an anticipated invasion by Napoleon Bonaparte, had crumbled to ashes. What on was he doing, he mused, in this distant God-forsaken corner of the British Isles, training, or trying to train, a bunch of incomprehensible, country bumpkins who couldn't even speak the King's English?

His family, back in Kent, were no doubt hoping that he would restore the family fortunes, bring credit to the family name once more, and allow them to rise to the top of society. Instead, here he was in Haddington, East Lothian, having been sent here by his colonel to bring the local "fencibles" up to an acceptable level of marksman's efficiency, sufficient to hold their own against the French army. He thought there was no chance of that.

He had tried to seek some measure of relief from his troubles in horse- racing. He was surprised to find that Haddington had its own horse-racing event, and had immediately put his name forward, as an experienced horseman, on the list of runners. If he couldn't win a simple flat race against a bunch of local yokels he would certainly give up altogether. Or so he reasoned.

His horse, Thunder, was a black stallion, standing at seventeen hands. Horse and rider knew each other very well by now. The opposition consisted of Billy Boy, a dark brown stallion, Popsy, who was little more than a pony, and Merry Maid, a white mare. The racecourse ran from Pencaitland Road end to Nisbet's farm.

At first, Thunder had led the field, but, after the turn at Nisbet's farm, Billy Boy had caught up and then passed him. Outraged Darnley dug his spurs into his horse's flank, while, at the same time, lashing out with his whip, not only at Thunder but also at Billy Boy. It was all to little effect, and, to loud cheers from the crowd gathered at the finish, Billy Boy was the winner. His rider received a handsome silver cup. Popsy, finishing last, was given a bag of oats.

Humiliated as he was, Darnley was taken even further aback by seeing Lady Elizabeth Rayner,

who lived in the large family mansion facing St
Mary's, warmly embrace the winner of the race,
one David Stewart, a local landowner and
farmer. Darnley had previously been introduced
to Lady Elizabeth at a welcoming party held by
the local council bigwigs. To say he was
impressed with what he saw was putting it
mildly. In his mind she represented the perfect
solution to his depression. Now that prospect lay
in ruins, too.

His reverie was interrupted by the realisation
that the rifleman, lying prone immediately in
front of him, was hitting the target with every
shot. Intrigued, Darnley beckoned to the
sergeant standing nearby.

 "What is that man's name, Sergeant?" pointing
to the rifleman.

"Rifleman Thomas Richardson, sir," replied the
sergeant.

"Have him report to me at the end of the exercise" ordered Darnley.

The bemused rifleman stood at attention in front of the mounted Darnley to whom an idea was already forming in his mind.

"Where did you learn to shoot like that?" asked Darnley.

"On my father's farm. Sir. A group of us farmers go out shooting regularly for crows, rabbits, anything we can find" replied the increasingly anxious rifleman.

"Do you know why we are here?" asked Darnley.

"Yes, sir" came the reply."To kill Frenchies, if they come over here."

"And what would you do if I told you that some of them were here already?"

"Why, sir. Shoot them as well, I suppose" replied an increasingly bemused Richardson.

"And what if I told you that a French spy was walking the streets of Haddington?"

"Point him out, sir, and I'll soon finish him off." said a, by now, eager soldier.

"I'll find him for you, never fear" said Darnley before wheeling his mount and trotting away.

At parade, next morning, Darnley put his plan into action. He had invited David Stewart to attend, prior to adjourning to the officers' mess for a pre-lunch refreshment.

While addressing the troops Darnley took the opportunity to remind them of the primary reason for their enlistment in the "fencibles."

"We are here to fight the French. But would you recognise one if you saw one?" he asked. "Does he look like this gentleman here?" nodding in David Stewart's direction, then winking at Thomas Richardson who was stood in the front rank of soldiers. This brought the intended laugh from the assembled men, except for Thomas who was looking intensely at David Stewart.

The following day was a Sunday. David Stewart attended the church service at St Mary's as usual, before mounting his horse, Billy Boy, and trotting along the river walk on his way to Lady Elizabeth Rayner's house.

He glanced over to the other side of the river. Next moment a shot rang out and he fell, mortally wounded, to the ground. Crouching behind a low wall on the river bank opposite, Thomas Richardson watched him fall, then hurried away. Darnley, meanwhile, was watching from the shadows. He turned Thunder's head away from the scene and trotted off.

People ran to the assistance of the stricken man from the church and from the Sands area.

"Who did it?" one asked the dying Stewart as he lay.

"I saw Thunder" he whispered and then fell back dead. His reply puzzled those around him.

"Thunder? You can hear thunder but you can't see it" said one.

Another smiled and answered.

"You can if it is a horse. Thunder ran last week in the Silver Cup race. His rider was an officer in the Fencibles."

Enquiries ensued and soon Darnley was being questioned about his movements. He vigorously denied any involvement in the incident. His men were also questioned. A totally confused Richardson confessed to the shooting. When asked who ordered the shooting he replied "No one. I shot him because he was a spy for the Frenchies."

He was further questioned on his reasoning but would say no more. Eventually he was charged with the lesser crime of culpable homicide and was sentenced to transportation to Australia.

Meanwhile Darnley attempted to resume acquaintance with Lady Elizabeth Rayner but was rebuffed by her, claiming she was in mourning over the death of Daniel Stewart.

Despite his protests his fellow officers became increasingly convinced that Darnley was the instigator of the crime. He was cashiered and sent home in disgrace.

CHAPTER EIGHT.

THE TOLBOOTH.

Below: a representation of how the old Tolbooth
would have looked.

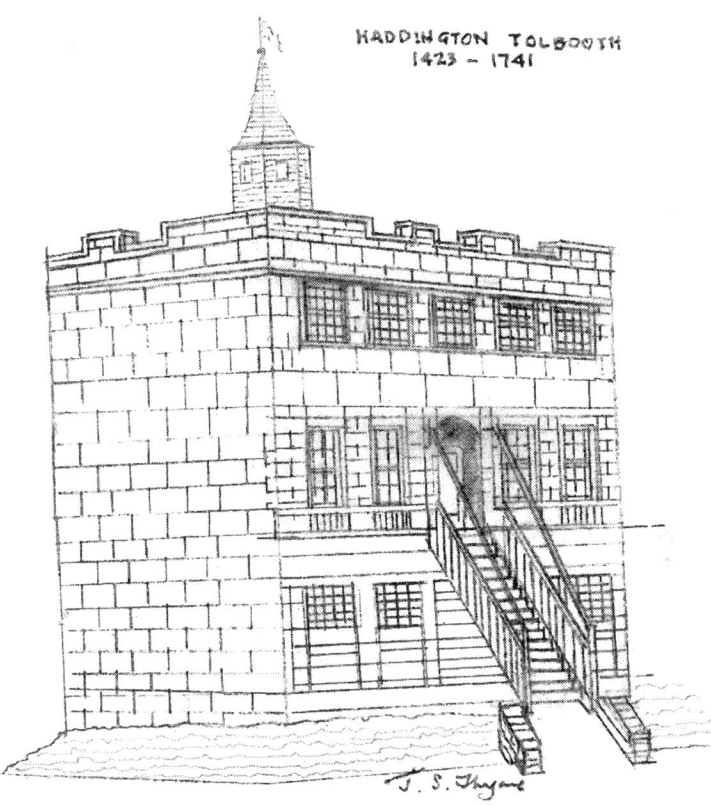

HADDINGTON TOLBOOTH
1423 - 1741

A side elevation showing the pit which lay under
the drawbridge.

THE TOLBOOTH.

St Mary's vied with the Tolbooth for the title of most important building in Haddington. The Tolbooth was used daily for over 350 years. Much of the history of Haddington, which is recorded in Council records for the fifteenth, sixteenth and seventeenth and early eighteenth centuries, revolved around it.

No painting, picture or early representation of the Tolbooth from those days exists today, but a physical description allows for some idea of what it looked like. It was a three storey, stone built building which was situated so that it faced Newton Port. It was topped with a steeple which housed both the town bell (used for heralding important events as well as the hours of the day), and a large clock which looked out on to Market Street..The top storey of the building was castellated, and both the roof and the steeple were tiled. A drawbridge led from the second storey to the street below. On the roof was a barbican, or battery, which was reached by a turnpike stair. A sentinel kept watch from here whenever danger threatened. The Town Council met on the first floor while the ground floor was used as a prison. The assize, or court, was held on the second, or top, floor.

The earliest available Council record is dated the 9th November, 1428 when : "this day Robert Tate appeared in court in the Tolbooth and sought information about the winding up of a land on the east side of Hardgate." Thereafter, mention of the Tolbooth is a regular feature of Council records on an almost daily basis. The early business of the Council focussed on land and property and established the physical development of Haddington on which much of the economy of the Burgh depended e.g. "1429. Bailey Tom of Ford, at the command of Peter of Sydserf, gave heritable possession of feu property to John Peter's son, shoemaker, in the form of a holding in the Sidegate,...paying rent to the Laird of Sydserf and his heirs, the sum of four shillings..."

Also featuring heavily in these early records are dealings with the Church. Significantly much of this activity focussed on the provision of alms for life e.g. "to the altar of St John the Baptist in the parish of Haddington" and "to St Mary the Virgin..."

Of course the daily business of running the town occupied the Council and caused them to devote special days to nothing else e.g. "Today it was ordered that the craft of smiths should keep their altar in good repair...

-ordered that the hangman shall confiscate all swine, dogs and cats that he finds running wild.

-ordered Sergeants to impose duty on all public mail.

-ordered that whoever fails to close the port gates shall pay an eight shilling fine.

-ordered that no one travels to Edinburgh with wheat, meal, beer or any other shipment of goods. Under penalty of being banished from the town and forfeiture of all goods for the town's use.

Security was always high on the agenda of Council business.

October 13th 1530. "The Council ordered that a suitable man be appointed to stand watch at every gate from 6a.m. to 9p.m., and one to keep the keys at night to admit neighbours who come in late, and, if strangers approach, to warn the baileys. Every one of the men to be given 6d per day. Any of them who fail in their service and make errors shall lie in the Thief's Hole for 24 hours and then be banished from the town.

To administer these duties required a body of men who could be relied upon to do their duty. Frequent appointment of burgesses, baileys etc.. occupied the business of the Council in the Tolbooth.

Life in Haddington was hard. Rewards were meagre and merely staying alive was an achievement. Inevitably there was constant recourse to the many taverns in the town, leading, equally inevitably, to argument, dispute and violence. The Assize Court was kept busy e.g. "John Thomson was ordered to pay Janet Darrow, spouse of John Patterson, as retribution for offences committed by him on her, the sum of ten shillings, before he could be released from the Tolbooth...he consented to be scourged throughout the Burgh, his ear nailed to the pillory post, and to be banished from the Burgh forever if arrested again"...

-"...those housed in the Tolbooth were required to pay 6d jailer fee on leaving"...

-"John Cockburn, wright, was accused of drawing his dagger at Henry White, proposing to stab him, having already stabbed William Crawford and been confined in the Tolbooth. He was fined £10."

-"John Ayton was accused of slandering the Provost, Baileys and Council...he called them all traitors, scoundrels and participants in the murder of the late James Ayton, his uncle. In point of fact, they were all innocent, and he duly confessed his guilt, saying he was drunk at the time. He was ordered to be detained in the Tolbooth."

-James Barns, bailey, lodged a complaint against George Fraser for negligence a) in refusing to erect a ladder at the bridge for the execution of John Thomson, common thief, and b) in forewarning John Cockburn...allowing him to escape...and avoid arrest for certain riotous behaviour and demonstrations of contempt. George Fraser was ordered to be detained in the Tolbooth while sentence was considered.

Life at the Tolbooth was never dull, but those in charge sought to enliven proceedings from time to time e.g. "John Wilkie, notary, was accused of showing contempt and slandering magistrates, plus persuading others to stay with him in the Tolbooth. He brought in pipers to play all night. That was the result of failing to keep the keys away from him. It was ordered that the Tolbooth doors should be locked shut all night as well as all day. John Wilkie was referred for sentencing. (26th September 1610).

"... because of the incompetence of the Tolbooth jailers, who had often allowed prisoners to escape, thereby leaving the Burgh without settlement of the debts they owed, the Council recommended, that a young, fit, able man be sought to be the Keeper of the prison..." (6/5/1682).

On the 20th January, 1683 "...The Council employed William Kennedy a Jailer and Keeper of the Tolbooth. His instructions were:

1-...he must provide sufficient security to relieve the Burgh from the damages incurred as a result of prisoners escaping.

2- An able-bodied, capable servant would be kept by the Jailer for whom he would be responsible. One or the other should be on duty at all times, from 6.a.m. to 10 p.m. when doors were closed and locked.

3- The jailer would receive prisoners and keep them in custody until ordered to release them.

4-All prisoners must first be booked into the Burgh Council books, kept by the Common Clerk, who would receive such booking money from the prisoners as decreed by the Council. Each prisoner to be charged four shillings a day.

5- No prisoner would be allowed to buy or bring any ale, wine, beer or other drink.

6- The Jailer and his servant must wear sword and scabbard at all times.

7- The Jailer and his servant must assist the Burgh officers when commanded by the Magistrates to arrest and imprison.

8- The Jailer must not allow anyone to carry arms into the Tolbooth, or anything else which could be used by the prisoners in helping them to escape.

9-The Jailer must not allow anyone to drink too much, or otherwise be incapable in the Tolbooth.

10- All prisoners were to be detained on completion of their sentence, until they had paid the jailer's fee.

11- No one was allowed to leave prison without a warrant from the Magistrate.

12- The jailer must obey the occasional orders and instructions of the Council.

Constant daily use, and being exposed to all kinds of weather, brought about the need for repairs. On the 3rd August 1691 (By which time the Tolbooth was approaching 300 years of age) ..."The Treasurer was instructed to repair the steeple of the Tolbooth, where the Clock and Great Bell were housed."

Workmen's advice was sought on the task i.e. whether to cover the roof with timber or lead slates, and how best to repair the windows in stone, timber and ironwork.

Nevertheless constant repairs were not enough. In 1741 a decision was taken to replace the Tolbooth – it having "become almost entirely ruinous." Subscriptions were collected and financial aid sought far and wide. A committee was appointed which decided to erect an entirely new building on a new site. That chosen was at the junction of the High and Market Streets, and eventually became the Town House. .

CHAPTER NINE.

WORLD WAR TWO IN HADDINGTON.

The outbreak of World War Two saw Haddington serving as a minor depot for military equipment. Reports of German air raids on London and the south east of England were sufficiently distant as to not ring any alarm bells amongst the town folk.

It was a considerable and nasty surprise, then, when, on the evening of the third of March, 1941, six HE (heavy explosive) devices were dropped by a German bomber, to land in a close proximity to each other in the Hardgate and Market Street area.

Five of the bombs exploded, causing extensive damage. One bomb landed within twenty yards of a packed New County Cinema. One fell in the rear premises of an ironmonger's in Market Street, another fell on Halliday's garage in Market Street. Bomb number four completely demolished Baillie's Gift Shop in Market Street.

At the time this shop was in use as a military equipment store.

Another bomb fell in the middle of the road in Market Street outside a draper's shop, and the sixth and final bomb ended up behind the main door of a dwelling house above a butcher's shop. This latter bomb did not explode and was eventually rendered safe by a Bomb Disposal Squad.

There were three casualties: Mr John Moggie, aged 35, Sergeant J.Mathieson and a private soldier, James Tyler who later died of his wounds. It was almost exactly 200 years to the day that the old Tolbooth was closed for business before being knocked down. The bomb that landed on Baillie's Gift shop would have demolished the old Tolbooth had it still been standing on that same site.

Those injured during the air raid included a fireman, a special constable and a civilian. Most of them had been struck by flying debris.

Several members of the public endured hair-raising incidents resulting in narrow escapes. A collapsed property meant that some had to be extricated albeit with cuts and bruises etc.. One husband and wife opened the door of their upstairs property only to find the stairwell had collapsed. They both fell heavily, leaving the husband badly injured and taken to hospital. His wife landed on top of him and suffered only minor cuts and bruises.

On the following day, several homes in the area were declared unsafe, prior to a thorough investigation, requiring some families to seek shelter. Arrangements were hastily made with friends and relatives so that no one needed to be sent to a rest centre. Damage to buildings in the area was quite extensive with many windows blown out.

Air raids continued in East Lothian until August 1942, but no more bombs were dropped on Haddington.

A Hurricane fighter plane crash in Haldane
Avenue.

AIRCRAFT CRASHES IN WW2 IN EAST LOTHIAN..

War in the air required replacement pilots at a terrific rate. Training was cut to a minimum in the race to put pilots in the air. The inexperience of pilots, the lack of properly developed flying control and navigational aids, and the looming presence of the Lammermuir, Moorfoot and Pentland ranges of hills, all contributed to a high death rate among trainee aircrew.

Many of them came from the Commonwealth countries of Australia, New Zealand, Canada and South Africa, so they were already unfamiliar with the area and the climate. Bad weather, especially the fog rolling in from the North Sea, took a heavy toll. Every type of aircraft was to be found in the list of fatalities – Spitfire, Hurricane, Typhoon, Mustang, Lancaster, Wellington, Blenheim, Beaufighter, Mosquito, Defiant and Beaufort. The wreckage of each and every one was to be found littered throughout East Lothian, from North Berwick to Humbie and from Tranent to Innerwick.

Over one hundred men (plus some women ferry pilots) were killed in flying accidents during the war years. Many of them remain in war graves in East Lothian cemeteries. St Martin's cemetery in Haddington alone, has 43 gravestones bearing the names of young men, with an average age of 23, from the Commonwealth who gave their lives for "the old Country."

When war came, events swiftly rendered previous carefully-ordered training planning redundant. The RAF simply did not possess a well thought-out, financially sound programme which would enable it to develop properly and meet war needs. Instead progress was erratic, reacting to events and forever imbued with an underlying feeling of panic.

Once the fighting started, and the head count of dead and wounded soared through the roof, there was an almighty rush to fill the pool of pilots needed. Inevitably the rush took a toll on training schemes. Young and inexperienced pilots were rushed forward to fill the gaps.

In peacetime, training was lengthy and intensive. Early basic training followed by learning how to fly, was followed by forty four weeks of thorough instruction in every aspect of aviation. A final six week stage was carried out by the Operational Training Unit, or OTU, which focussed on the conduct of warfare in the skies. Once war started, this latter stage lasted just two weeks. Indeed some went directly into war service from training school, which was now down to twenty two weeks, without going near an OTU.

On the ninth February, 1941, Flight Lieutenant P.A.Burnell-Phillips crashed his Hurricane fighter in Haldane Avenue, Haddington (see picture) the burnt out remains of his aircraft lay only a few yards from a back garden. This was the only occasion when an aircraft crashed in Haddington.

There were thirty two crashes, involving fifty eight fatalities in East Lothian.

CHAPTER TEN.

MODERN MURDER.

The Haddington of today is widely regarded as a peaceful market town which is very different from the much larger Edinburgh which lies sixteen miles away to the west. Violence is not associated with Haddington's much slower tempo. It is surprising to discover that this is far from the case. On at least four occasions in recent years a murder has been committed. When neighbours have been questioned as to their reaction to a horrific incident which has taken place nearby, they invariably express amazement that such a thing could happen.

"This is a quiet street. Things like that don't happen here."

If only that were true!

Take the first case. An East Lothian man, Charles McCue, murdered a six year old Haddington girl in 1972. He pleaded insanity, a plea which was accepted and resulted in him being committed to Carstairs Hospital for the criminally insane. He spent twenty one years there before being transferred to the Royal Edinburgh Hospital, where he spent a further two years before being released under supervision.

Incarceration did not have the beneficial effect intended. On the contrary McCue was not inclined to pursue a normal, crime-free life. Instead, in 1998, he was again accused of two breaches of the peace involving minors. He attempted to pervert a twelve year old boy by showing him indecent pictures and magazines, before trying to induce the boy to expose himself in exchange for money.

He further tried to persuade a fifteen year old girl to go to bed with him in order to perform sex acts. His plea of not guilty was refused. The Sheriff would not grant bail but instead sent him for trial. He was remanded in custody pending sentence which was deferred while waiting for crown, social inquiry and psychiatric reports.

Earlier, the mother of the children involved had claimed "He seemed such a nice man. He took the children to a local show and let them take the wheel of his car on waste land." This followed an earlier meeting with McCue whom they saw collecting scrap metal from a skip. He offered to split the profits if they would help him, having first consulted their mother. Gaining the children's trust and confidence, however, only made the offence more serious.

Victoria Terrace in Haddington was the setting for another murder in July1999 although there was no premeditation on the part of the assailant.

Keith Adams, 38, an ex-boxer who shared a flat in Victoria Terrace with Kirsten Jones, 29, told the court that the couple had argued over an alleged association he had with a barmaid. Kirsten accused him of his infidelity even after they had returned to the flat.

"She just started shouting and hitting me" he claimed. "I just remember putting my hand around her neck and grabbing her." She collapsed, and, in a panic, he tried to hang himself from the rafters in his bedroom. Police later found ladders leaning against a wardrobe, and a belt looped around the rafter.

Notwithstanding his plea of panic following what he felt was more of an accident, Adams was in his local pub just a few hours later. He did voluntarily present himself at a local police station to confess.

Pathologists said that Kirsten, a slightly built girl, probably died as a result of the pressure Adams had put on her throat. The jury, in Edinburgh's High Court, found him guilty of culpable homicide. He was jailed for seven years, a verdict which Kirsten's mother, Mrs Jean Moncrieff of Haddington, described as disappointing.

The 19th March, 1998, was the date of the following murderous event which took place in Monkmains Road, Haddington. It was the familiar tale of a broken marriage causing untold distress among the young family of two sisters, Stephanie and Kerry, and brother Ryan. The mother, Clare, was an alcoholic and split up from her husband Daniel Janworski, leaving Stephanie, aged 15, to effectively take over the running of the household. Older sister Kerry, aged 18, was a care worker who had a growth deficiency which made her look much younger.

Stephanie found it all too much. After discussing the situation with Ryan, she told him Kerry had to go. Playing truant from Knox Academy, she took to drugs and strong drink. Kerry complained and tried in vain to make her sister give up her dangerous lifestyle, which included spending the night with a twenty four old man. The two sisters argued incessantly.

Eventually, on March 19th, Stephanie and friend Sheree Hunt agreed to go on a shopping trip to Edinburgh, although both should have been at school. Sheree arrived to meet Stephanie at 9 a.m. and found her in her bedroom. She was told "We are going to murder Kerry" by Stephanie, picking up a dressing gown cord as she spoke. She told her friend Sheree to play some music so that she would not hear what happened. Sheree told the court "I heard a scream and realised something was going on." She ran downstairs and saw Stephanie on Kerry's bed with Ryan beside her.

Kerry's face was ashen, her eyes staring. Sheree fled not knowing whether Kerry was alive or not. She later phoned and was told by Stephanie "Yeah. I done it." They met in Haddington a half hour later where Stephanie said "I don't know what came over me. How could I do such a thing to my own sister?"

Stephanie and Ryan then took £60 from an ATM using Kerry's card. They went to Edinburgh and had lunch, then bought cigarettes and a new pair of trousers for Stephanie. She claimed to have found Kerry's body on her return.

While in custody awaiting trial, Stephanie wrote a boyfriend, saying "I was in a pissed-off mood. I was sick of her trying to run my life and just basically being a pure bitch to me. I didn't mean to go that far. I only wanted to give her a fright."

Her defence lawyers argued that she should be found guilty of a less serious charge of culpable homicide on the grounds of diminished responsibility. The jury took a different view and found her guilty of murder. Judge Lady Cosgrove imposed the mandatory sentence of detention without limit of time, with a recommendation she should serve at least six years.

Ryan admitted he and his sister had discussed killing Kerry but thought it was just a joke. He was cleared of murder after it was found there was insufficient evidence against him.

According to a psychologist, who examined Stephanie, she was a very sad, unhappy little girl.

"Although she tries to appear a capable, confident, sixteen year old woman, inside there is still a very damaged and hurting young girl." Fate was not kind to Stephanie. At a difficult time for teenagers she was thrust into the position of leader of the household. It was all too much for her. Something had to give. Unfortunately it was her self control and a basic recognition of right and wrong that gave way.

Finally, on the 15th March 2013, Brian Bathgate, a joiner and carpenter who worked for Raywood Construction, a Tranent builder, was found dead in the living room of the cottage where he lived , alone, at Barney Mains on the outskirts of Haddington. His body lay for two days before his brother called, having been unable to reach him by phone.

At first detectives suspected that the severe wound to the neck, sustained by Bathgate, was self inflicted. Forensic evidence, however, caused them to change their minds and instead suspect a murder had been committed.

Witnesses and neighbours called Bathgate a placid, polite man, who always gave a friendly wave when addressed by passers-by. He had originally had his wife and family of four children with him, but, latterly was living alone.

Detectives continued their investigation by questioning neighbours to see if they had seen anything or anyone suspicious. Cattle farmer Willie Kerr, of Barney Mains Farm, said "...have taken my CCTV footage which covers the road coming up. They'll know every vehicle that came up or down that night."

Enquiries continued for over two years, and then, on the 10th December 2015, Gordon Veitch, 56, from Tranent, was found guilty of killing Brian Bathgate. He had visited Bathgate on two occasions to argue with him. For some reason, known only to himself, he ended the second meeting by plunging a knife into Bathgate's neck before leaving.

Forensic experts, using footprint analysis, were able to trace Veitch because of his distinctive walk in which his right foot pointed outwards. He left bloody footprints in the cottage where Bathgate's body was found. He had previously approached the cottage, in the early hours, by walking across fields, rather than down the approach road.

His advocate, John Scott Q.C., said "Veitch is receiving treatment for cancer and it is doubtful if he will survive the sentence of 16 years passed on him." But Detective Chief Inspector Keith Hardie said "He showed a callous disregard for the life of Brian Bathgate. Only he knows why he decided to murder Mr Bathgate during what appears to have been an unprovoked attack. He has shown no remorse for his actions, or any consideration for Mr Bathgate's family and friends."

It would be a relief to believe that this case was the final murder to take place in Haddington. However realism, with regard to the vacillations of human nature, persuade us that such is unrealistic and unlikely.

Brian Bathgate.

Brian Bathgate was found dead in his home at Barney Mains Farm

Gordon Veitch.

CONCLUSION.

Haddington occupied a prominent position in the economy of Scotland right up until the beginning of the seventeenth century. When James VI of Scotland moved to London to become James 1st of England, he took with him his courtiers and all their hangers-on as well. When this act was combined with the silting up of the south bank of the Forth estuary, it heralded a decline in the trading with Europe, especially the Netherlands and the Baltic states which Haddington had enjoyed for centuries. Aberlady ceased to be a significant port.

Later with the increasing importance of Glasgow and trading with the Americas, it seemed that Haddington's fate was sealed.

The decline was halted in the nineteenth century when there was a huge rise in the trade of grain and grain products. Haddington became the centre for market trading. The Corn Exchange was built in 1854 and immediately saw brisk business. The Hiring Fair, in which farmers came to Market Street every Friday to hire men to work in their fields, drew large crowds. Wheat, corn, barley and oats all flourished in East Lothian fields. The opening of the rail link to Edinburgh, and thence to all parts of the United Kingdom, saw grain and its products distributed worldwide. The railway station dates from 1844 and did not close for over a hundred years.

In the twentieth century Haddington assumed its former prominence by becoming the county town of East Lothian. The headquarters of East Lothian Council in John Muir House became the head office of the largest employer in the area.

The expansion in housing in Haddington in the last quarter of the twentieth century, and continuing into the twenty first, saw the population of the town rise to ten thousand. At the same time, the opening of the new A1 highway to Edinburgh has made travelling to this city much easier. Hence Haddington is in

danger of becoming merely a commuter town
for the Capital.

THE END.

INDEX

R

S

Made in the USA
Columbia, SC
15 June 2017